Scene 1   A Moor

Enter Coll alone.

Coll. Lord, the weather is cold, and I am Ill-wrapped;
I am numb with the cold, so long I have napped;
My legs totter and fold, my fingers are chapped.
Times are bad on the wold, and my life is all lapped
    In sorrow,
  What with storm and tempest,
  In the east, in the west.
  I get no rest
    Midday or morrow.

We luckless farmers that work on the moor
Can hardly keep the wolf from the door.
With things as they are, no wonder we're poor,
For our land is as bare of crops as the floor.
    Lord love us!
  We are so abused,
  Over-taxed, ill-used,
  We are sadly confused
    By those above us.

They give us no rest, by our Lady I vow,
These lords' men. I'm blessed if I understand how
They can say that it's best not to plough the land now.
We are all so oppressed they will hardly allow
    Us to live
  Always holding us under
  While they bluster and blunder.
  It is no wonder
    We cannot thrive.

Maybe one will come now, for example, to borrow
My cart and my plough, and I, to my sorrow,

Must let them both go, or I'll suffer tomorrow.
So 'tis every day they drill us and harrow
    Us mercilessly.
    And if I refuse?
    Well, what's the use?
    Put my head in a noose?
        No, thank you, not me!

For if a man's preferred to a lord's suite nowadays
None dare say a word except in his praise.
None can be heard to find fault with his ways,
And no one, I'm sure, believes what he says.
    Though a liar,
    He eats of the best;
    He can brag and boast,
    And all at the cost
        Of men that are higher.

It does me good as I stray, like this, on my own
Of this world to say what I think, and make moan.
But I must up and away or my sheep will be gone.
There they are. While they stay, I'll sit on this stone.
    No doubt,
    Though the moors are lonely,
    I'll have company
    If there be any
        Others about.

Enter Gib, who does not see Coll.

Gib Eh, eh! Lord bless us! What does it all mean?
      Why are things so much worse than they've ever been?
      Lord, these winds are spiteful, and the weather is keen;
      The frosts are so frightful my eyes water. Day in
          Day out,
        Now in dry, now in wet,

The Wakefield Second Shepherds' Play

FROM THE TOWNELEY CYCLE.

Modernized version

by
Benn Sowerby.

Order this book online at www.trafford.com
or email orders@trafford.com

Most Trafford titles are also available at major online book retailers.

© Copyright 2009 Benn Sowerby.

All rights reserved. No part of this publication may be reproduced, stored in a retrieval system, or transmitted, in any form or by any means, electronic, mechanical, photocopying, recording, or otherwise, without the written prior permission of the author.

Printed in Victoria, BC, Canada.

ISBN: 978-1-4269-1137-8 (Soft)

We at Trafford believe that it is the responsibility of us all, as both individuals and corporations, to make choices that are environmentally and socially sound. You, in turn, are supporting this responsible conduct each time you purchase a Trafford book, or make use of our publishing services. To find out how you are helping, please visit www.trafford.com/responsiblepublishing.html

Our mission is to efficiently provide the world's finest, most comprehensive book publishing service, enabling every author to experience success. To find out how to publish your book, your way, and have it available worldwide, visit us online at www.trafford.com

Trafford rev. 11/20/2009

North America & international
toll-free: 1 888 232 4444 (USA & Canada)
phone: 250 383 6864 ♦ fax: 812 355 4082 ♦ email: info@trafford.com

By the same author

Poems

Mandragora
No Garlands
A Word in Silence
Thule
Monologue
Rhymes

Novel

Fright in the Forest

Biography

The Disinherited (the life of Gerard de Nerval)

Guide Books

Guide to Cambridge
Guide to Oxford
Guide to Stratford

The Wakefield Second Shepherds Play

Now in snow, now in sleet,
With my shoes frozen to my feet
    Things are hard, there's no doubt.

But as far as I can see, or yet as I go,
Such poor husbands as we have nothing but woe,
Trouble and worry. It's always so.
Our hen, Capil, now, she struts to and fro
    And cackles,
  But if she once croak
  Or begins to cluck,
  Woe to our cock,
    For he is in shackles.

Ay, men that are wed cannot do what they will,
But must go where they're led, for good or ill,
And nothing said, but follow until
At last they are dead and can lie still.
    We live and learn.
  A man, though clever
  Once hooked, will never
  Be free again ever,
    And now it's my turn.

But now late in our lives - a marvel to me
What fate contrives for our destiny;
I'd ne'er have believed such wonders I'd see, -
Some will have two wives, and some men three
    Or more!
  Some are sad that have any,
  But life's not worth a penny
  To him who has many;
    Of that I'm sure.

But young men a-wooing, if you'll only be taught,

Beware of wedding and first take thought:
It's no good saying "If I'd known ..." once you're caught.
Endless regretting's the price of such sport.
    You'll grieve,
If you have your way,
As surely, I say,
As night follows day,
    For as long as you live.

By Saint Paul's epistle I've a wife by my fire
As sharp as a thistle, as rough as a briar;
Her eyebrows bristle; she's a sour-faced leer.
Once she's wet her whistle she can sing right clear
    Her Pater Noster.
She's as huge as a whale,
She's a gallon of gall.
Heaven help us all!
    I wish I'd run till I lost her.

Coll. Gib, look over the bank! Were you grumbling or sleeping?

Rising up.

Gib. Eh! A plague on your pranks, hiding and peeping!
Seen Daw anywhere?

Coll.   Heard him blow, I'd say
Somewhere over there, and coming this way,
    Not far.
    Stand still.

Gib. Why?

Coll.   I hope he'll come by.

Gib.   With some startling new lie
If we don't take care.

Enter Daw, who does not see the others.

The Wakefield Second Shepherds Play

Daw. Now may Christ's cross speed me, and Saint Nicholas!
Of that I'm in need; all is worse than it was,
If one only takes heed, but let the world pass:
It's slippery indeed and brittle as glass,
    As I've found.
  This world was never so sore
  Bewildered before
  With wonders more and more
    All around.

Never since Noah's flood were such floods seen,
Winds and rains so rude, and storms so keen;
Some stammered, some stood betwixt and between.
Now God turn all to good! I say and I mean.
    For ponder:
  These floods so many drown
  Both in fields and in town
  And bury all down,
    That it is a wonder.

We who wander o' nights to take care of our sheep,
We see sudden sights, when other men sleep.

He catches sight of the others but does not address them.

  My heart missed a beat. What can those two mean?
  Some mischief, no doubt. I'll pretend I've not seen,
    Slip away.
  But what if they should
  Be here for my good,
  Perhaps give me food?
    So, then, I'll stay.

  Good sirs, I think we are happy to meet.
Addressing the others.

Benn Sowerby

    Please give me a drink and something to eat.
Coll. If you ask what I think, you're a lazy cheat.
Gib. What, dinner and drink. Why, then, take a seat
    Till we've made it.
   Will you have a plate?
   Though the fellow came late
   Yet he's in fine state
    To dine, if he had it.

Daw. Such servants as I who work day and night,
  Must eat our bread dry, and that is not right.
  We're often wet and weary while our masters sleep tight;
  And who's there to worry if we don't get a bite?
    Who's to say
   When pay-day comes round
   Some fault won't be found
   And then I'll be bound
    They'll dock us of our pay.

  But now I swear true, whatever you can spare,
  I'll promise to do some work for my fare,
  Though work as I would I'll still feed on air,
  For I never yet knew a full stomach here.
    But why fret?
   And why should I worry?
   I'm not in a hurry.
   I can wait for my curry
    A little while yet.

Coll. You'd be a fine one to serve a poor master.
  You'd soon make his money run faster and faster.
Gib. Peace, boy; have done. We've no time for a waster.
  We've our work. It's all one to us if you fast or
    Go hang.
   Where are our sheep boy? We yawn.

Daw.	Sir, this day at dawn
	   I left them in the corn
	      When the matin bell rang.

	They have pasture eno'. They cannot go wrong.
Coll.	That's good. But oh, these nights are long. Yet before we go let us have a song.
Gib.	Yes, that's what we'll do to cheer us along.
Daw.	I agree.
Coll.	I'll sing the tenor, I.
Daw.	And I the treble so high.
Gib.	Then the bass falls to me. Are we all ready?

They sing.

Enter Mak, wearing a cloak over his clothes, soliloquizing.

Mak.	What a life this is, if life it's worth calling. A man has no peace for bickering and brawling; At home all he hears is brats squalling and bawling; And now to top this here's a caterwauling. What's to do?
Coll.	Who is this that sings such a song?

Mak.	I am doing no wrong,
	   Merely strolling along.
	      Who are you?

Gib.	Why, Mak, is that you? What are you doing here?
Daw.	Is it he? Ho, ho! We'd best look to our gear.

Snatches cloak from Mak.

Benn Sowerby

Mak I warn you, you rogue, you'd best have a care,

Pretending not to know them.
　　　　For I'd have you to know I'm a lord's messenger
　　　　　　And a yeoman.
　　　　　　Fie on you! Get hence
　　　　　　Out of my presence.
　　　　　　I must have reverence
　　　　　　　From such low men.

Coll. Why, Mak, so quaint? We know who you be.

Gib. Mak playing the saint? That's something to see.

Daw He can act well, I grant, for a rogue such as he.

Mak. I shall lodge a complaint. You'll be flogged, all three.
　　　　　　If not worse,
　　　　　　For causing a breach
　　　　　　Of the peace.

Coll. 　Mak, I beseech,
　　　　　　Don't talk in that southern speech;
　　　　　　　Get off the high horse!

Gib. Enough of this, Mak! I've a good mind to beat you.

Daw. If you don't know us, a whack might be able to teach you.

Mak. Why, good friends, alack! I am happy to greet you.

As if suddenly recognizing them.
　　　　I'm quite taken aback.

Coll. 　Yet how often we meet you!

Gib. 　　　Rogues are cheap,
　　　　　　And so late afoot
　　　　　　You might be out for loot
　　　　　　When by common repute

       you're a stealer of sheep.

Mak. Yet I'm true as steel, and they wrong me who say 't,
There's a fever I feel that's come on me of late,
Which I try to cool by strolling at night.
My stomach's not well; I'm in a bad state.
    Therefore
      Full sore am I and ill.
      As I stand here stock-still,
      I've eaten not a gill
        This month and more.

Coll. And your wife, I'd enquire, how does she do?

Mak. Sits all day by the fire with a noggin or two,
And the brats in full choir keep her company too.
She hasn't a care, but that's as you knew;
    And then
      She eats three times her share,
      And every year
      A new child she'll bear
        And sometimes a twin.

Even if my purse were as heavy as stone
She'd eat me out of house and of home.
Of all the foul race of women I've known
There was never a worse than this old crone.
    I confess
      Should she die tomorrow
      It were no great sorrow
      And I'd willingly borrow
        To pay her a mass.

Gib. There's none so worn-out in all the shire.
I would sleep for a bout if 'twere not for my hire.

Benn Sowerby

Daw. I am cold in these clouts. I wish we'd a fire.

Coll. I'm weary, I vow, trudging round in the mire.
   Wake, now!

Gib. Nay, down I must lie
   And shut my eye.

Daw. I'm as ready, truly,
   As any of you.

 But, Mak, you lie here. Between us you'll be safe.

Mak. Then I can't help but hear what you say; so in faith
   Take heed.
  From my top to my toe

Saying his prayers.
   Manus tuas commendo,
    Pontio Pilato.
     Christ's cross me speed!
  Now's the time for a man to seek what he would,

Rising while the rest sleep.
  And creep quietly in to the sheep-fold.
  Nimbly to work, then, but not too bold,
  For I risk a bad bargain if the tale should be told
   In the end.
   Now's the time to steal.
   But he needs good counsel
   That would come off well
    Who's no money to spend.

 So about you a circle, as round as the moon,

He puts a charm on the sleepers.
  Till I've done all I will; so until it be noon
  May you lie stone-still. By then I'll have done.

The Wakefield Second Shepherds Play

So I lay my spell. Sleep soundly each one.
    On high
  Over your heads my hand I raise
  So that sleep may now close tight your eyes
  And I may have time to gain my prize
    Before you can spy.

Ho, ho! They sleep hard, as ye may all hear.
So much for the shepherds! Now what's there to fear?
If the flock be scared, I'll call out "Who's there?"
As if I've Just stirred. Here's promise of cheer
    For tomorrow;
  A fat sheep this, I'd say,
  And a good fleece, I'11 lay.
  When I can I'll repay,
    But now I must borrow.

Exit with sheep.

Scene 2   Mak's House.

Mak speaks outside the door.

Mak. Gill, Gill, are you in? Get us a light.

Gill. Who makes such a din at this time of night?
I've just sat down to spin, and I mean to sit tight.
If I'd a fortune to win I'd not stir a mite.
    So it is all day.
  If I'm called at all hours
  It's beyond my powers
  To finish my chores.
    Be off, I say!

Mak. Good wife, open the latch. Don't you see what I bring?

Gill. Is it you? Then I'll pull the catch. Come in, my sweeting.

She opens the door and he goes in.

Mak. You don't worry much if I'm kept waiting!

Gill. A sheep! For such you're likely to swing.

Seeing the sheep.

Mak.   Nay, nay!
  I am worthy of my meat,
  For in a strait I can get
  More than they that toil and sweat
    All the long day.
This one fell to my lot. Gill, it's my lucky day.

Gill. Let's hope you will not be hanged for it.

The Wakefield Second Shepherds Play

Mak.   Nay,
        I've escaped, Gillot, many times in a fray.

Gill.   "But so long goes the pot to the water" they say
           "At last
              It comes home broken".

Mak.   Let it not be spoken!
        But by the same token
           Come, help me fast.

        I wish he were basted. I'm ready to eat.
        It's a year since I tasted good sheep meat.

Gill.   If they come ere he's roasted, the sheep may bleat -

Mak.   And then I'd be toasted. I'm in a cold sweat.
        Go bar
        The front door.

Gill.   Yes, Mak!
        I'll have the whole pack
        Before long at my back;
           They'll suspect me for sure.

Gill.   I've a trick we can try. Don't stand there and groan.
        Look! Here we will hide him until they're gone,
        In the cradle beside me; a child new-born
        They'll think they've spied. Now leave me alone.

Mak.   Good, good!
        And I'll tell them at dawn
        A child was born.

Gill.   As pretty a bairn
        As ever I bred!
        Never despise a lucky cast.
        A woman's advice always helps at last.
        Before anyone spies now off with you fast.

Mak.   I'll he there ere they rise despite the cold blast,

Benn Sowerby

      And asleep.
May they sleep, all three!
I'll creep in quietly
As 't had never been I
    That carried off their sheep.

Scene 3   The Moor.

Coll, Gib, Daw and Mak are awaking.

Coll. Resurrex a mortuis! Give me a hand!
Judas carnas dominus! I can hardly stand.
My foot sleeps. Alas! It seems part of the ground.
And, to make things worse, I'm as hungry as a hound.
    Aie, ee!
Lord, but I've slept well!
I'm as fresh as an eel,
And as light I feel.
    As a leaf on a tree!

Daw. Bless me, what have I seen? Ah, how my head aches!
What a fright I've been in! I still shiver and shake.
I near jumped out of my skin. For heaven's sake
What can it all mean? Wake, fellows, wake!
    We were four.
    But where is Mak now?

Coll. We were up before you.

Gib. He's not moved, I vow.
    He went nowhere.

Daw. I dreamed he was wrapped in a great wolf-skin.

Coll. I've a wolf as it's happed, not outside but in.

Daw. I thought while we napped he went with a gin
And a fat sheep trapped, but he made no din.

Gib.   Be still.

Benn Sowerby

          You're daft with dreams, lad.
          It's but a fancy you had.

Coll.   Now God turn all to good,
          If it be his will.

Gib.   Get up, Mak, for shame! You sleep too late.

Mak. What? Who called my name? Ah, by my faith,
       My leg has gone lame. I cannot stand straight.
       And my neck is the same. I've a crick in it. Wait!

One of them twists his neck.
          That'll do.
       I had bad dreams all night
       That put me in a fright.
       I'll be in a sorry plight
          If they come true.

       I dreamed my wife, Gill, as I walked on the wold
       Had been off to call a new sheep to our fold,
       And, truth to tell, another child
       Would be to cap all, more than we can hold.
          With a house full
       Of young mouths to be fed
       And little enough bread
       I'd be better dead.
          Fare you well!

       I must go home, by your leave, to enquire after Gill.
       You may look up my sleeves; I've nothing to conceal.
       And I hope you'll believe that I would not steal.

Exit.

Daw. Good riddance to the knave! Let's hope all's well
        This morn
        And we have all our store.

Coll.   I'll go before.
        Let us meet.

Gib.   Where?

Daw.   At the crokked thorn.

Scene 4   Mak's House.

Mak speaks outside the door.

Mak. Undo the door! Hey, there! How long must I stand?
Gill. What a noise is here! Bad luck to the man!
Mak. Ah, Gill, what cheer? It is I, Mak, your husband.
Gill. Just as I feared ! Bad news travels fast and
       Alone.

She opens the door and he enters.
       Here he comes now, and all
       Out of breath, too! Well,
       Am I never to call
          A moment my own?

Mak. What a fuss she makes! And yet all she does
     Is to sit all the week twiddling fingers and toes!
Gill. Why, who watches and wakes? Who comes and who goes?
     Who brews? Who bakes? Who mends the hose?
       So then,
     If the truth he told,
     Whether young or old,
     Sad 's the household
       That lacks a woman.

     But what luck have you had with the shepherds, Mak?
Mak. The last thing they said as I turned my back
    Was they'd look that they had all their sheep, the whole flock.
     I think they'll be mad when they find they lack

The Wakefield Second Shepherds Play

        A fat wether.
        But howe'er the game goes
        They'll suspect me, I suppose,
        And make a great noise,
            Shouting "Mak" all together.

But you must do as you said.

Gill.   I agree to, still.
       Swaddle him up to the head here in the cradle.
       To be on the safe side and make things more real,
       I'll be ill in bed. Come help me!

Mak.   I will.

Gill.   Soon
         Coll will be here
         With Gibb in the rear.

Mak.   If they find the sheep there
           I'm as good as done.

Gill.   Watch well till they come. The baby's asleep.
       I've wrapped, him up warm. He can scarcely peep.
       Sing a song now to charm the wee thing and keep
       Him free from all harm. When you hear them rap
           On the door,
        Sing "Lullay, lullay"
        As loud as you may.
        If I give you away
           Never trust me more.

Scene 5   The Moor.

Enter Coll, Gib and Daw.

Daw. Why, Coll! has a ghost scared you out of your bed?
Coll, Alas, I'm so crossed, I could wish I were dead.
A fat wether we've lost.
Daw. What's that? God forbid!
Gib. Some thief, to our cost, has done this foul deed.
Coll.   But who?
I have searched without sleep
All Horberry Steep
And of fifteen sheep
Found only one ewe.

Daw. Think what you will, by Saint Thomas I swear
Either Mak or Gill was in this affair.
Coll. Peace, man, you speak ill. Of slander beware.
Ye were out on the hill; when he left I was there.
Take heed.
Gib.   Well, that's as may be.
But I'd make so free
As to swear it was he
That did this same deed.

Daw. To go there 'tis best, and knock on his door.
I'll never break crust till I find out for sure.

The Wakefield Second Shepherds Play

Coll. Find him we must. I'll not drink before.

Gib. And I'll never rest until we know more.
  Come, then.
   However it be,
   You can take it from me
   I'll not sleep till I see
    Him again.

Scene 6   Mak's House.

Mak and Gill within, she in bed, he singing. Enter Coll, Gib and Daw outside the door.

Daw. What a noise they make! He's crooning, for sure.

Coll. I've never heard such a racket before.
Call to him.

Gib. Mak! Undo your door!

Mak. For pity's sake! Who's that out there
  That makes such a riot?
  Who is it I say?

Daw. Honest folk we be.

Mak. Good fellows, I pray
  Keep your voices quiet.

My wife's ill in bed in here, and Lord knows
I would rather be dead than we had any noise.

Gill. Send them off with all speed, for every sound goes
Right through my head. I might get some ease
  If they'd go.

Coll. What, Mak! Turn us away?
How are you, I say?

Mak. You in town today?
  Well, how are you?

Lets them in.

You have run through the mire and are still all wet.
I'll make you a fire if you'd like to sit.
I suppose I've to hire a nurse now. More yet!

The Wakefield Second Shepherds Play

      My dream was no liar, for this is it
         In due season.
      Like the old dame in the shoe
      I don't know what to do.
      But we must drink as we brew,
         And that's plain reason.

    But you're for the road and want something to eat.

Gib. We're not in the mood for liquor or meat.

Mak. Is some bad news abroad?

Daw.   A sheep lost this night,
      And stolen, not strayed. Our loss is great.

Mak.   Come, drink!
      If I had been there,
      Some would have paid dear.

Coll.   Some say that you were,
         And that's what we think.

Gib. Mak, for all that one knows, it might have been ye.

Daw. Either you or your spouse, and so say we.

Mak. Now if you suppose it was Gill or me,
      Come, search the house, and then you will see
         For my share
      There's no sheep, live or dead,
      In house or in shed.
      And Gill, my wife's been in bed
         Since she lay down there.
As I am true and leal, to God here I pray
May this be the first meal I shall eat this day.

Coll. Now, Mak, think well what it is you say.
He learned early to steal who could not say nay.

Gill.   Again they start.
      Out, thieves, begone!

Benn Sowerby

                You come to rob us of our own.

Mak.   Don't you hear her groan?
            It should melt your hearts.

Gill.   Away, thieves, from my bairn!   Don't you dare to go near.

Mak.   If you knew what she's borne, your hearts would be sore.
        You do wrong, I warn you, in coming before
        A woman so worn with labour. Beware!
            Ah, my middle!
        I pray God so mild
        If ever I you beguiled
        I may eat this child
            That lies in this cradle.

Mak.   Peace, woman, for God's sake, and cry not so!
        You make my head ache. I am filled with woe.

Gib.   Our sheep's killed, I take it. What d'ye find, you two?

Daw.   It's no use to look. We may as well go.
            Only rags and tatters;
        I can find no flesh,
        Salt nor fresh,
        Nor any cooked dish,
            Only two empty platters,

        No live creature but this, tame or wild,
        And stronger than this no bairn ever smelled.

Approaching the cradle.

Gill.   It's not so. God bless and give me joy of my child!

Coll. Our aim was amiss. We have been too bold.

Gib. Sir, we have done!
　　　　Our Lady bless the day!
　　　　Is your child a boy?

Mak. It would give a lord Joy
　　　　To have him for a son.
　　He kicks when he wakes. It's a joy to see.

Daw. I don't doubt he takes after you merrily.
　　But tell me what folks his godparents be?

Mak. There came for our sakes -

Coll. Hark, now, a lie.

Aside.

Mak. 　　And I give them thanks,
　　　　Parkin, and Gibbon Waller, these two
　　　　And gentle John Horne; it's true
　　　　He made a to-do
　　　　　With his great shanks.

Gib. Well, Mak, we agree from now on to be friends.

Mak. No pleasure to me. I get no amends.
　　Goodbye, all three, none too soon for my ends.

Daw. Fair words there may be, but no love attends
　　　　This year.

The shepherds start to leave.

Coll. Did you give the child anything?

Gib. Why, no, not a farthing.

Daw. I'll go back with something.
　　　　Wait for me here.
　　Mak, I hope you believe I mean well by your child.

Benn Sowerby

Returning into the room.

Mak. I should know you deceive by the way you smiled.

Daw. The babe will not grieve. He is so mild.
    Mak, with your leave, let me give your child
        A sixpence.

Approaching the cradle.

Mak.   Go away. He's asleep.

Daw.   I think I see him peep.

Mak.   When he wakes up he'll weep.
       I beg you go hence.

Daw. Let me give him one kiss, and lift up the clout.
    What the devil is this? He has a long snout.

Seeing the sheep.

Coll. He's all fashioned amiss. There's some mischief about.

Joining Daw.

Gib. As the sire is, so the young will turn out.

Joining them.

       To my mind
       He's just like our sheep!

Daw.   What, Gib? Let me peep.

Coll.   So nature will keep
       Always in kind.

Gib. Well, upon my word, what a wicked deceit!
    'Twas a real fraud.

Daw. A foul cheat!
    To the stake with this bawd and bind her fast.
    Such a false scold will hang at the last,
       And so shall you.

To Mak.
>See how they swaddle
>His four feet in the middle.
>I never saw in a cradle
>>A horned lad before now.

Mak. Peace now awhile! Do you dare scorn?
     He is my child, by this woman born.

Coll. What shall he be called? Mak's heir will be shorn.
     We have been beguiled by a trick. He's forsworn,
        I say.
     A finer child than he
     Never sat on woman's knee,
     So pretty to see,
        And merry as May.

Daw. I know him by the ear-mark. That's good to go by.

Mak. I tell you, sirs, hark, his nose is awry.
     He's bewitched. Ask the clerk; he'll not tell you a lie,

Coll. This is false work. Revenge, say I.
        Fetch a weapon.

Gill.   He was taken with an elf -
     I saw it myself -
     When the clock struck twelve
        He was misshapen.

Gib. They're as like as two pies; there's no more to be said.

Daw. Since they stick to theor lies they deserve to be dead.

Mak. If e'er again I steal ewes you may cut off my head,
     But now on my knees I beg mercy instead.

Benn Sowerby

Coll.   Friends, as I think, it's
   No use for us
   To swear and to curse;
   So without more fuss
    Let's toss him in a blanket.

They toss Mak in a blanket.

Scene 7   The Moor

Enter Coll, Gib and Daw.

Coll. Lord, but I'm sore. I am ready to burst.
     I can't go a yard more. I must lie down and rest.
Gib. As a sheep of seven score he weighed in my fist.
     I could sleep anywhere, but sleep I must.
Daw.   Well, then, pray,
        Lie down on this turf.
Coll. I still think of that thief.
Daw. What good to grieve?
        Do as I say.

They lie down to sleep. Enter an angel who speaks to them.

Angel Rise, shepherds, attend, for now He is born
     Who shall take from the Fiend what from Adam was shorn;
     The Devil to confound, this night He is born.
     That God is your friend on this happy morn
         He attests.
        To Bethlehem go see
        Where now lies He
        In a crib lowly
          Between two beasts

Exit.

Coll. That voice as finer than any I've heard
     Such a marvel we've seen as would make a man scared.

Gib.	Of God-in-Heaven's Son he brought us word.
	A great light shone, when he appeared,
	All about.
Daw.	He spoke of a bairn
	In Bethlehem born.
Coll.	That star is the sign.
	Let us seek him out.
Gib.	That was a song to bring us good cheer.
	All the air rang.
	Such tones sweet and clear,
	And not a note wrong, 'twas a wonder to hear.
Coll.	My voice is strong; I can sing you the air,
	You shall see.
Gib.	You think you're in tune
	When you're baying the moon.
Daw.	Hold your tongues! Have done!
Coll.	Well then, later maybe.
Gib.	To Bethlehem he said we should go this day.
	Already we've made too long a delay.
Daw.	Let's no more be sad, but merry and gay
	We'll do as he bade and be on our way
	Without any noise.
Coll.	Let us, then, hurry,
	Though we're wet and weary,
	To that child and that lady;
	We've nothing to lose.
Gib.	In times gone by there were learned men,
	David, Isiah, and others akin,
	Who did all prophecy that in a virgin
	He surely should lie to pardon our sin
	And win favour
	To save mankind from woe,

>   For Isiah said so:
>   Ecce virgo
>   Concipiet a saviour.

Daw. Now happy are we, alive this day
That saviour to see, for whom we pray.
Lord, 'twere well with me for ever and aye,
Might I kneel on my knee, some word to say
   To that child.
   But the angel said
   He was poorly arrayed
   And in a crib laid,
      Lowly and mild.

Coll. Patriarchs there have been and prophets before
That desired to have seen this child that is born;
They are long gone with their hopes forlorn.
We shall see Him, 'tis shown, ere it be morn,
   By the star's token.
   When I see Him, 0
   Then I shall know
   That all is so
      As prophets have spoken:

That to poor men as we are he would first appear
As would be declared by his messenger.

Gib. On, then, let us fare; the place is not far.

Daw. We are all prepared. Let us follow in fear
   That bright star.
   Lord, though we be
   Ignorant all three,
   Grant now that we
      May bring Him cheer.

Scene 8 - A Stable in Bethlehem.

Coll. Hail, comely and clean! Hail, young child!
Hail, Maker, born of a maiden so mild!
A match Thou hast been for the Devil so wild;
The beguiler of men now himself is beguiled.
    See, how merry He is,
    See, He laughs, the sweeting!
    A right happy meeting!
    I bring Thee my greeting
      And a bob of cherries.

Gib. Hail, sovereign Saviour! For us Thou hast sought,
Hail, noble flower that all things hast wrought!
Hail, full of favour, that made all from naught!
Hail! I kneel and cower. A bird I have brought
    From afar.
    Hail, tiny lad!
    Thou art the head
    Of all our creed,
      Little daystar.

Daw. Hail, darling dear, full of Godhead!
I pray Thee be near when I have need.
Hail! Sweet be Thy cheer! My heart would bleed
To see Thee sit here in so poor a shed
    With no pennies.
    Hail! Here is all
    I can bring Thee, a ball
    To have and play withal
      And go to the tennis.

Mary. The Father of Heaven, God omnipotent,
    Who all nature governs, his Son has sent.
    May our sin be forgiven by this advent.
    I conceived Him even as was God's intent,
        And now He is born.
      May He keep you from woe!
      I shall pray him so.
      Spread the news as you go,
        And remember this morn.

Coll. Farewell, our Lady, so fair to behold,
    With thy child on thy knee!

Gib.   Alack! how cold
    He lies here. Now we must go back to the fold.

Daw. In truth already it should be told
    Far and wide.

Coll. What grace we have found!

Gib. With glory is He crowned.

Daw. And we are bound
    To sing it aloud.

They go off singing.

Printed in Great Britain
by Amazon